The Master Plan

STEVE BALDERSON

Special discounts are available on quantity purchases.
Contact the publisher at office@dikenga.com for details.

Dikenga Films | Books | Audio
www.dikenga.com

ISBN: 978-1-7354569-8-0

"People mistake chaos for productivity."

- Clark Balderson
(My Father)

"We wouldn't know what order was unless we had messes. It's the contrast of order and messes that order itself depends upon."

- Philosopher Alan Watts

"Darling, never use the word neurotic to describe yourself. Use the word thorough."

- Movie Star Karen Black

CONTENTS

INTRODUCTION

When I was planning the shooting schedule for my third feature film, I instinctively went about it in a way that, at that time, I had no idea hadn't been done before. After years of practicing this new concept, and sharing it with others, who have also implemented this model, now I know. Which is why I'm sharing it with you in this book.

My first two feature films were fantastic experiences. Both during production and afterwards when each film was distributed worldwide and won awards and critical acclaim. While my overall memory of those shoots two decades later is generally positive, if I focus more intently into what each shoot was really like, I recall how exhaustive and draining they were – physically and mentally.

Whether you go to film school or not, no amount of reading, studying, or theorizing will prepare you for the realities of directing an actual film. There are too many variables in the real world which often come together on a film set in a melodramatic fashion when you least expect them. And usually, they happen all at the same time.

Never mind how many car chases there are, or blazing explosions, even hairpulling and blood-drawn catfights—all of which happen behind the scenes, regardless of what your movie is about—there is only one all important element to every film shoot. No matter if it's a feature film, short film, music videoclip, or a commercial. All of them connect and come together in the framework by which each is organized. It isn't your budget, your cast, your crew, or even your script. It's your daily shooting schedule.

The schedule of your shoot will determine everything about your production. It determines whether or not you remain on budget. A poorly organized schedule might cause last-minute rewrites which could cross the fine line between having a good, finished film or a really lousy movie.

Most films are shot out of order. You might start your shoot by filming a scene that takes place in the middle of your movie. Or, likewise, you might end your shoot with the first scene. Usually, films are organized based on locations and availability of cast and crew. This makes it even more important to make sure your schedule is solid, since you'll usually be filming non-sequentially, which has the potential to be confusing.

Traditionally, filmmakers used a big folded production board, or stripboard to arrange their shooting schedules. A stripboard was typically made from a super durable and strong cardboard. Accompanying the board were dozens and dozens of super-skinny color-coded thinner cardboard strips, each detailing the information of every single scene in your entire script, which could be inserted into the stripboard and arranged to your desired order of filming. Some stripboards ended up being six or eight feet long depending on the length of the shoot. My first films were all scheduled using a stripboard, and I really loved the process of making them – which I've since evolved and will get to later.

Production boards and strips were very expensive. So much so that when I realized the absurdity of the price, I decided to make my own version from recycled cardboard boxes, colored paper and duct tape. Worked fine and cost next to nothing.

Eventually, computer software programs made it possible to do the same thing but without wasting so much paper. They, too, are incredibly expensive, so if you insist on scheduling your movie virtually, you might consider an excel spreadsheet or even an online document that people can access in the cloud.

All of these earlier methods might be well and good for scheduling your shoot theoretically but none of them implement the most important element. Time. Actual time. The time on a clock. The Master Plan uses this element, which up until now it seems, no one in the entertainment business has ever considered.

I never intended to keep it a secret because I know how much it could help people. After working with me, most of my Assistant Directors have implemented the features of The Master Plan into their next production schedules. All of them have concurred it has totally revolutionized their shoots. Every AD who has worked with me reported a significant increase in efficiency which helps them remain on schedule and finish at or under budget.

When I started using The Master Plan, I found that not only did we stay on time and at or under budget, but that we also never exceeded a 12-hour workday. So, I began announcing that we would never exceed a 12-hour workday on the very first day of filming. On one feature in particular, which was a made-for-TV movie for Mark Cuban, I promised my cast and crew we would never exceed a 12-hour workday. The Production Manager, Line Producer and other Producers panicked and told me I could never promise such a thing as it would be impossible. "Just impossible!"

The cast and crew also looked skeptical and, while hoping it would indeed be the case, their past experiences on other film sets with endless days and shorter turnaround times left them doubtful my Master Plan was as great as I said it was.

I'm aware that to the skeptics it sounds too good to be true, but because I've lived it, I know it's true. Belief isn't something that appeals to me. Experience appeals to me. If something is a truth of the universe, then it is possible for people to experience it. I understand and know that until people also have the chance to experience it, they won't believe it. Even if they want to.

Usually, it takes about four or five days before the cast, crew and producers realize the magic. On the movie for Mark Cuban, I don't think it really sunk in for the cast and crew until the shoot was over. We averaged being ahead of schedule and wrapping each day at just about 10 hours. Once we wrapped at around eight working hours.

If you don't believe me, ask the cast and crews connected to any of my films. They will all attest to it. If you don't want to do that, maybe you might try it out for yourself and find out what happens. Again, it isn't important you believe me. It's important that you simply implement The Master Plan into the way you go about scheduling your shoots. It will enhance your experience on every shoot and keep all of them as enjoyable as possible. With or without the behind-the-scenes melodrama.

Some of the ingredients in assembling The Master Plan are similar to the traditional methods. If you're a seasoned pro, you might not think you need to read about breaking down a script and so forth. I encourage you to do so as one or two major steps are not part of the earlier scheduling methods. For the first timer, I'll guide you through my entire process from start to finish so you can know how to implement each step.

For the sake of this process, pay no attention to what your budget is. The Master Plan can be utilized on any size budget. And if you love working 14-hour days, that's fine. You can still implement The Master Plan so that each 14-hour workday can be the most rewarding and enjoyable as possible. All that said, The Master Plan is most valuable to the filmmaker on limited resources. I developed it because I wanted to make sure I was being as organized and efficient as possible on my film sets. If you are a studio head with endless resources, it might mean very little to you. Still, even if you have a 20-million-dollar budget, utilizing The Master Plan might make it possible for you to achieve the desired results as if you were working with 30 or 40 million.

ORGANIZATION

Once I directed a film in Macon, Georgia during the peak of late summer humidity. The air was so thick you could cut it and spread it on your morning toast. It was my first film project to be produced outside of Kansas, and I fell in love with the town and its people. As a resourceful budget-minded producer and filmmaker, I'm always looking for any way to keep the cash resources as untouched as possible.

One idea I came up with was called the "Adopt a Star" program. It would allow a local wealthy patron of the arts a chance to sponsor one of the actors from the film: movie star Karen Black (Five Easy Pieces, Nashville, Great Gatsby, Day of the Locust, Firecracker), Rock-n-Roll Hall of Famer Jane Wiedlin (The Go-Go's), cult icon Mink Stole (Serial Mom, Heathers), and The Princess of Hollywood Pleasant Gehman. The wealthy sponsor would host the actor, feed the actor, and drive the actor to and from the set, and so on. It would allow that sponsor the opportunity of a lifetime and also save our production thousands of dollars we would otherwise have to spend on doing all of the above.

Out of the Adopt a Star program I developed the "Host a Lunch or Dinner" program. I designed a Meals Signup Sheet to pass around to the people who signed up in the Adopt a Star program, as well as other socialites and well-to-dos in Macon. On the signup sheet were a list of our production days and the times we'd be taking lunch or dinner breaks. Whomever wanted to host a lunch or dinner at their mansion or restaurant of choice, could simply fill in their name next to the time and date of the meal.

Also listed in columns next to the time and date was information about the total headcount for each meal followed by the number of people who can eat anything, how many people have food allergies, and if there were any other food related restrictions to consider. No matter what our cast and crew headcount was, each meal that was sponsored could have fed an army. I'm so grateful for the generosity and openness of these hosts to feed us and invite us into their homes.

Though my wishes were to keep lunches alcohol-free, several hosts insisted, "Oh, one or two won't hurt anybody." And on the other end, so long as we were wrapped for the day, alcohol could be offered at dinner. It was a wonderfully fun and great way to immerse ourselves into the culture of the place. I thought, even if you don't have movie stars in your movie, all film productions shooting on location should have a Meals Signup Sheet passed around to the locals.

One aspect of the sheet that hadn't originally occurred to me was the influence of social peer pressure, or one host's desire to "outdo" another host. By passing around the Meals Signup Sheet on one piece of paper, each new potential meal sponsor would clearly see all the other people who had already signed up. I overheard one of them say, "Well if Mr. X is doing Tuesday, I'll do Wednesday and it'll be epic, so none of y'all will remember what he served."

Soon we had each lunch and dinner catered, sponsored, hosted or claimed for throughout our entire production schedule. Including additional meals and pool party barbecues that people wanted to sponsor on our days off. It was awesome and while saving the production a lot of cash, we were able to really know Macon, its people, and its way of life.

Being organized and having a solid plan helped achieve this experience.

We knew what time lunch and dinner breaks would be for every single day. The hosts were advised the cast and crew would arrive either on time or within 15-minutes either side of that time.

By mapping out and planning for each mealtime, we were able to give Carolyn the opportunity to sign up for Friday dinner at 7:30pm, say, instead of lunch because she had a nail appointment.

In order to have an idea of when mealtimes would be, we had

to know what we'd be shooting, where we'd be shooting and how long it would take us to drive everyone from our set to Carolyn's house.

And in order to know all that, we'd first have to have a concise daily schedule to indicate each step of the process from script to screen.

On many filmsets, catering is brought to the set. This saves the most time because people don't have to go anywhere. And depending on where you're filming, it might be wiser to have meals on the set even if it costs a little more for the delivery fee. In our case, we needed to save every dollar we could. Macon is a modest sized town, and it only took five minutes to get to and from each of the sponsored meal locations.

HAPHAZARD HAZARDS

In contrast to that experience in Macon, once I was hired as a director for a production which was filming in Los Angeles. Los Angeles is a congested and sprawling metropolis where, depending on the time or day, it can take 20 minutes to drive three miles.

On our first day of production, lunch was to be taken at 1:00pm. I was shocked when the producer walked up to me at 10:30am and asked, "What should we do for lunch?" Days earlier I had emailed the producer my food preferences, assuming that as with any production, meals would be planned and organized by the producer ahead of time. When I'm not the producer, I respect the producer and don't want to overstep any boundaries. And when I am the producer, I know what needs to be done. My mistake was assuming that the people involved also knew this.

The hours that followed were made up of distractions which

kept the crew from doing their work. In the middle of a task, each person had to stop what they were doing, walk over to a PA holding a laptop, scour a menu that had far too many choices, and place an order. In order to scroll through the menu, only one person could use the laptop at a time. It was a very inefficient use of time, and very quickly the production was behind schedule.

The consequences of being disorganized can lead to disaster on any film set—no matter the size of the crew or scope of the budget. The importance of being organized is paramount. I cannot emphasize this enough.

BUDGET

Earlier I mentioned that my desire to save production cash is what led to developing the "Adopt a Star" and "Meal Sponsor" programs. Being organized and having a comprehensive production schedule certainly goes hand in hand with having a thorough budget. No matter the cash value of the budget you're working with, the amount of cash you intend to spend directly relates to your schedule. Likewise, the schedule you create will directly influence the budget.

I'd like to take a moment and point attention to the word BUDGET. When I use the word, I don't always mean cash. There are many "costs" in film production which happen in kind, or resources that are borrowed or found, or donated. Those meals which were sponsored in Macon, Georgia have a value, which is part of the budget, even though not a cash value. When making the thorough schedule and comprehensive budget for any film, every single element must be considered. The big items like shelter, food and safety, and every little item such as masking tape, batteries, and toilet paper. Each element must be thought of and explored when putting together a budget and schedule.

Feeding people is an integral part of the budget. It was only when I examined the cash cost of doing so, and what we would sacrifice from other areas in the budget which also needed to be addressed, that I came up with the sponsoring concepts. I knew in order to make the most out of the cash resources we had, I should try and get as many meals donated or sponsored as I could.

While budget and schedule go hand in hand, for the sake of this book, I will stick to the topic of scheduling. Periodically you will see a "Budget Side Note" incorporated which directly relates to the topic we'll be discussing, but I won't be getting into specific details here.

WHY HAVE A SCHEDULE?

Have you ever heard someone tell you how much they love having a terrible night's sleep? Or someone who brags about being so stressed out they can't think straight?

Maybe you know someone who loves feeling miserable, but I don't. So, I'm going to go out on a limb and suggest that it is likely that no one enthusiastically wants to be stressed. It's highly likely that no one consciously hopes for a terrible night's sleep.

Being organized reduces stress and increases productivity. Being less stressed also helps you sleep better. While exercise is a benefit, simply being organized improves your chance at achieving your desired weight.

The more organized you are when thinking about what groceries to buy, the probability is you'll choose items that are good and nutritional. If you wait until you're starving to decide, it'll probably be too late to think, causing the "grab and eat whatever is closest" mindset. To be in that mindset at that moment of chaos is to be unconscious. Meaning that, in that moment, there is no conscious thinking about whether the food being consumed has any nutritional value.

Being organized generates consciousness.

Being aware of what it is you're doing.

Planning ahead for what it is you will be doing.

A lot of people I know who prefer avoiding a schedule somehow mentally connect having a schedule to not having any fun. It's as if they think that being organized might destroy any chance of spontaneity and living in the moment.

Whether or not you sometimes think those things, I'm here to tell you that it is totally possible to have a schedule, be productive, well organized, and have a lot of fun. You can, indeed, have both! You can still take long walks into the wild, spend lazy days at the pool, or beach, or take hikes in the woods. You can still finish your screenplay, edit your book, shoot your film and plan for the next creative endeavor. All at the same time. So long as you're organized and have consciously planned for it, it can be done!

A TIME TO IMAGINE

Let's start with a finished script that will likely not be altered in any way with additional revisions or drafts. The shooting script. Whether you have written it or someone else has – you'll need the script before you're adequately able to make a shooting schedule.

Now that you have your script, the first step is to envision it. What is your plan for how to convey each scene or sequence visually?

If it's a film I'm going to direct, I usually start with sketching storyboards and making shot lists for my Cinematographer (sometimes called the Director of Photography, DP or DOP). Sometimes I do this while I'm reading. My mind processes things entirely visually. The images, colors, camera angles and rhythm of the edits are vividly clear in my mind's eye. As I explained in my book *Filmmaking Confidential*, the only perspective that matters at this moment is the one which comes from within—YOUR

INDIVIDUAL PERCEPTION.

The purpose for planning how you'll film each scene or sequence will inform you how much time it will take to execute. Some scenes can be executed very simply, while others are complex and will take a long time.

If your scene is set at a restaurant and shows a man and woman talking at a dinner table, your plan might be to have a static camera on a tripod, and shoot a wide two-shot, single close-ups of each actor, followed by a few over the shoulder shots, and maybe some coverage. Coverage in this case might be a closeup of the woman's hand reaching for a glass of wine. This kind of scene is fairly simple to execute, even if the dialogue is filled with emotional intensity from your actors.

Now, if you are planning to shoot that same dinner scene with an elaborate dolly move choreographed to capture the specific moment in which the woman grabs her glass of wine and hurls it at the man's face, well, that's going to take a very long time. Not only will it take many tries before all the choreographed elements line up, you'll also need to re-set or re-stage everything you see in the scene after every single take. The man's wine-soaked face will need another chunk of time back in the hair and makeup chair. His wine-soaked costumes will need to be switched out with clean ones. You'll also need to replace the tablecloth. And on and on.

All of this information will be very useful when you are arranging the shooting schedule for that scene. So, as you visually imagine each scene and sequence from your script, take some of these things into consideration.

If you do not like to decide how to shoot a scene until you arrive on set, you will likely find that you will be behind schedule fairly quickly. Now, I'm not suggesting you have to storyboard all your scenes. It might be just as efficient to make a basic shot list so that when it comes time to break down the script and begin the scheduling process, you'll know what your plan is.

If you are having trouble envisioning your script, you probably aren't meant to be the director. If you cannot envision your script and insist on remaining the director for the project, my advice is to immediately team up with a DP who can envision it for you.

In either case, teaming up with a DP as early as possible is key. Once I've finished my storyboards or shot lists, I get together with my DP and visually walk through the entire story.

Sometimes the DP is inspired by a scene and wants to try an elaborate and complicated camera move which could take an entire afternoon to accomplish. That's fine. Knowing this ahead of time will allow you to plan for it in the schedule. If you wait to decide this on the day of shooting, when you have already scheduled other things, it'll be an unwelcome surprise.

The ending beach scene in Alfonso Cuarón's Roma (when actress Yalitza Aparicio walks out into the waves) took a very long time to film. Part of the challenge was to make it appear as though that sequence was captured in just one shot (which it wasn't), and it's one of the most breathtaking moments in cinematic history. Be careful. It is possible to dismiss a complicated idea because it takes time to execute. Sometimes visually complex scenes are incredible and important for your film.

If you're on a limited budget and happen to also be the screenwriter with some filmmaking experience, you might want to limit the number of locations, explosions, car chases or nail-biting catfights while writing your script. All of these things eat up a lot of time and money. If you have a lot of money and spending significant amounts of time on one of these complicated sequences is exactly your goal, that's fine. Regardless, you want to have an understanding of what it takes to accomplish the scene in question – no matter what the context.

If you've never filmed anything before, how do you find out how long something takes to shoot? Ask your DP. Hopefully you've teamed up with a DP with some experience. The DP can estimate how long something will take and share that with you.

The specific amount of time varies based on each individual DP's cinematographic style, their speed of movement in between takes and their personality type. Once I worked with a DP who wasn't especially assertive nor a very good leader. Without any kind of guidance and structure, his team would often take three times as long to accomplish a set up than it would take most any other crew. It came as no great surprise that we were frequently behind schedule. It was one of my first films and I didn't yet know how important it is to have this conversation ahead of time. That tiresome experience is also one of the things which pointed me to develop The Master Plan.

No matter how long your DP estimates it will take to prepare a shot, it is good to find out so you can plan for it. There is no such thing as a good or bad amount of time. However, if you are operating with a limited budget and your DP says he or she can manage to set up and execute only three shots per day, it might make sense to hire a different and more efficient DP.

To build a thorough Master Plan you will need to already have a DP in place so you both can discuss your approaches to executing each scene and sequence in the script.

I like to build my shooting schedules based around my personal likes and dislikes. I've heard that Clint Eastwood operates his film sets in a similar fashion—basically working from 9am to 5pm. Give or take. I like a call time to be around 8am with a wrap time around 6-7pm. For me it is very important to have a good solid workday and also make time to have healthy and substantial meals plus a great night of rejuvenating sleep. I don't want to be awake filming all night long and then feel lousy the next day. And since I don't want to experience feeling lousy, I'm certainly not going to ask anyone else to have a lousy experience either. That's just rude.

Anyone who thinks they need to push their crews to work more than 12 hours as a means to communicate to your financiers or producers that you aren't wasting their money is ridiculous.

By keeping your workdays between 10-12 hours long you'll notice an improved quality of work from your cast and crew. Good sleep also makes people more alert. It's a proven fact that good sleep will result in your cast and crew working more efficiently. Their efficiency and productivity will actually save time in the long run. Whereas longer hours don't always mean you'll accomplish any more than you would have in less hours.

There is also something to be said about safety. When people have had little to no sleep and are entrenched in hour 14 on set for the third day in a row, many mishaps and accidents are likely to happen. Mishaps and accidents take up time and cost money.

Most experienced cast and crew will demand a 12-hour turnaround. This means that at whatever time you wrap shooting, the next day's call time to arrive on set cannot be any earlier than 12 solid hours from that wrap time. It's good to practice this even if it's your first time on set and you're running on adrenaline with excitement and want to keep going and going and going. Not everyone on your cast and crew will be as passionate or as excited as you.

Lack of sleep impairs your ability to think, focus on any situation at hand, learn anything and remember whatever it was you learned. Those first few adrenaline-filled days will eventually catch up with you before your shoot is finished.

Why bother making life on set miserable when you could otherwise just add an extra filming day? If you don't have the budget for an extra filming day, then it is even more imperative that you build a solid Master Plan and are as organized as possible before ever setting foot on the set.

Before you read on make sure you:

__ Have completed your script

__ Have completed your storyboards or visual concepts

__ Have discussed how you and your DP will film and capture each sequence

__ Learn the speed by which your DP operates in the world

__ Have understood the time it will take to adequately capture the scene, reset it, and do additional takes

PREPARE FOR A BREAKDOWN

My father says, "People mistake chaos for productivity." Having anxiety, stress, running around like crazy, pulling your hair, talking and breathing really fast, yelling at people, and generally behaving like you're insane doesn't accomplish anything. Other than the accomplishment of presenting yourself to be a lunatic. There is nothing efficient about behaving this way

The amount of energy expressed by the person I describe above is energy that isn't being spent actually accomplishing a task. It takes a lot of energy to behave like that. It also causes more anxiety and stress than you had when you began behaving that way.

I never learned to behave that way when being productive and thus my brain isn't wired to behave that way when doing so. So, when I'm accomplishing a task, I do it without waving my hands around and behaving like a crazy person. There's no stress.

WHAT IS A BREAKDOWN?

Does it require hours of therapy and medication? Maybe. But in this case, we're not talking about a breakdown you have, we're talking about a breakdown that you make.

A breakdown is the process which will prepare you for a film production. It is a comprehensive report and evaluation of a screenplay which identifies every element you will need in order to produce and film the script.

Your breakdown will happen early in the development of your film. The information gathered from the breakdown process will dictate how your production is scheduled as well as budget needs.

For clarification:

The act of budgeting is the process of sorting your dollars and other resources into categories. Because a budget is an entirely different entity, though similar in process to create, we will not go into that here.

The act of scheduling your production is the act of sorting all the pieces you will need in order to plan it efficiently.

WHEN DO YOU MAKE YOUR BREAKDOWN?

Once you have locked your script.

Locking your script freezes every scene and page number.

Make sure before you lock your script that you have numbered all your scenes and are satisfied with everything about how it was written. Everyone involved in the project has added their ideas, all the edits and rewrites have been made, and the script is finished.

Each film in production evolves three times. It begins as the film you've written (the script). It evolves into the film you will shoot (production), where things will change no matter how hard you try. The final stage of evolution comes with the film you edit (post-production), which will be different than either of the two previous incarnations.

Sometimes the scriptwriter labels the locations differently from one scene to the next. Before you lock your script, go through the scene headings to make sure that each is accurately labeled.

Likewise, sometimes there are characters present in the dining room that don't say anything or react in any way as to be mentioned in the prose. Imagine you're watching this scene on screen. You'll want to make note of any characters who appear in the scene when you know them to be present even if they aren't specified in the writing.

In order to lock your script, you don't need to be satisfied with the final edited version of the film you've shot, because you are obviously not there yet. You only need to be satisfied that the script is in a solid place you feel good about, in the event it miraculously ends up being exactly what was written on the paper. It won't, of course. Just make sure that if it ends up exactly as written that you are satisfied.

Even though you've "locked" your script, you still have the freedom to change something. In the software I use, if something is cut or rewritten, the existing page numbers and existing scene numbers remain the same. Therefore, if these changes take place after the breakdown process, there's no reason to worry. You'll only have to update the breakdown sheets for the scenes which have been rewritten.

Traditionally rewrites are then included in the script as A, B and C pages and sometimes with a different color (pink pages, blue pages, and so on).

Once you've locked your script you are ready to do a breakdown.

Each scene in your script contains valuable information:

Where does the scene take place?

Is it night or day?

Who's in the scene?

Characters with names, background actors without names, passersby, and so on.

Are there any special props mentioned?

Any specific sets or costumes mentioned?

What about vehicles?

Anything that might require visual effects?

Hopefully there aren't any children and animals, but if there are, know you're in for a treat!

NOTING THE ELEMENTS

First, go through the script and highlight or circle or underline all the components that make up each scene.

You will need to assign colors and a language for easy understanding. You might decide that a pink highlighter is used to identify people, a green highlighter is used to identify cars, and a yellow highlighter is used to identify props. You might decide to circle visual effects or explosions or underline animals. It doesn't matter what you decide to do and what colors you use. Just make sure you keep that strategy from start to finish.

By the end of this process, your script will be either colorful or full of fun shapes, or both!

Next, you'll want to put all of this information down on paper. Or in the computer. Each scene will require a different breakdown sheet. Only one breakdown sheet can be used for one scene. Two sheets cannot be used for the same scene – unless they are being filmed in two totally separate moments or locations involving time travel, say. Let's continue by assuming that your script is a standard narrative with a standard structure.

Each scene gets its own special breakdown sheet.

You can use actual breakdown sheets on paper or computer software – it doesn't matter. Use whatever works best for you.

I prefer to use colored notecards for my breakdown process. If you decide to use notecards, you will be able to skip the next step in the process. Please read the next steps thoroughly before you decide to actually begin your breakdown process so you can find out which method might work best for you. If you are a beginner, it might be more beneficial to use a breakdown sheet so you can become familiar with the process.

My first two films used breakdown sheets, physical stripboards, and I loved it. It was so much fun gathering all that data. It was when I developed the Master Plan that my process altered slightly. For the sake of understanding how everyone else does it, know that it's a fun process.

HAVING A BREAKDOWN

Now it's time to dig deeper. Whether or not you see a therapist, practice meditation, yoga, or exercise, it's important to have a clear perspective when it comes to scheduling your film shoot. Having clutter in your mind will hinder the process. However, the following is about your script having a breakdown—not you.

Did you know there is no such thing as a problem? It's true. The only thing that truly exists is your reaction to a situation. Most humans make challenging situations into problems, but you won't need to. Examine your reaction to the situation and use creativity and resourcefulness to respond to the situation.

Our next step is to properly breakdown each scene and sequence with the information gathered from both your screenplay and storyboards or visually conceived shot lists. This is where the previous two steps come together.

You can do this by using an archaic production stripboard, expensive computer software, post-it notes, or free computer software. I like to use colored note cards. There is no right way or wrong way to do this. My advice is to investigate each method and find out whichever way works for you and use that.

For the sake of explaining this, I'll illustrate my process using colored note cards. If you're using a stripboard, the same information we put on the note cards will need to be included on each strip. Likewise, if you're using computer software, you'll need to include each element from the note card onto each line of your spreadsheet. If you are using computer software, you might find that there are some key pieces of information to enter and not find a place to record this data. This is because the software wasn't designed or engineered with these elements in mind. Perhaps if you work for a magic movie scheduling company who designs said software, it would be a good idea to take the information in this book and incorporate it so the software can evolve for the better.

Transfer all the information from the Visual Storyboards and Breakdown Sheets into notecards or strips so that each card or strip has the same information that the Breakdown Sheet and storyboards have on them. Notecards are smaller and easier to sort and arrange and rearrange.

If you want to, you can give your script a deeper breakdown than I do at this stage. I try and stick to only the basics which will have an impact on the shooting schedule. General props or specific set dressing notes don't impact your shooting time unless they require special effects or an explosion.

Take your script and start at the beginning. The first scene, for example, reads: Int. Bedroom – Day. This tells me to grab a yellow notecard.

I work based on the most typical combinations of colored notecards, which is usually made up of colored cards in yellow, green, blue, purple, and pink. You can assign whatever colors you like to whatever meaning you like just so long as you stick to that arrangement in an ongoing way. If I buy an assortment of cards made up of yellow, green, blue and purple colors, I assign them like this:

- Yellow = day, interior
- Green = day, exterior
- Blue = night, interior
- Purple = night, exterior

I use the pink cards for the day/date, a pickup day or a location move. For now, set the pink cards aside.

Going back to the script and our first scene, I take the yellow card. In the top left-hand corner, I write the scene number. Then on the top line I write the location name. In the body of the card, I write a short description of what happens in that scene. In this case, I write "he wakes up with her." Then I jot down, on the right side of the card, the characters who appear in the scene. Oliver and Evelyn. If there is any kind of special effect or notable time-impacting element, I list that at the bottom of the card.

Because a number takes up less space than writing out the character's name, if you have a lot of characters, each character should be assigned a number. Usually, your main characters are "1" and "2" and "3" and the supporting characters follow with "4" and "5" or however many. Now, if a movie star is in your movie and plays a small part, they might be assigned to "Number 1" even if they aren't the main character. This hierarchy has more to do with the amount of money the movie star was paid, a contractual obligation, or just plain ego stroking.

In the top right-hand corner, I write down the amount of time it will take to execute that scene. This data will stem from the conversation with your DP based on your storyboards and Visual Breakdown.

On average, it takes me one filming hour per one page of the script. So long as I'm working with a cinematographer who is organized, efficient and skilled. And a talented cast of actors who are as equally prepared and skilled.

My favorite cinematographer to collaborate with is Hanuman Brown-Eagle. When we're working on a project together, we discuss everything ahead of time. We are each so incredibly prepared by the time we walk on set there's almost little else to say to each other. Of course, the architecture and the way the natural light is flowing into the space might inspire me to change our shot list. This oftentimes makes my previously sketched storyboards obsolete. But Hanuman is so prepared and skilled that any such changes rarely alter our schedule.

Your average filming time will vary based on your personal experience and how you interact and work with your DP, and how your DP interacts and works with their crew. There is no right way or wrong way. There only is what is. So, if you average two filming hours per one page of the script, that's fine. Knowing the speed by which you like to work is helpful.

In this case, going back to our script, the first scene in the bedroom is half a page in length. There is no dialogue, only action. Normally I would write down "30 mins" in the top right-hand corner. Which includes set up time as well as actors performing while the camera is rolling. In this case, it's about a man who wakes up to find that his wife has died in her sleep. My intention was to make it a single shot and to allow the camera to roll uninterrupted in real-time. Hanuman and I planned to shoot a few variations on the same shot. Taking all this into consideration, I decided to write down "90 mins."

Later when we were filming and working with the incomparable actor Xander Berkeley in the role, we ended up successfully completing several variations on the opening shot in about 45 minutes and were already 45 minutes ahead of schedule for the day.

Once you have combined the basic data from the Breakdown

Sheets and Visual Breakdown Storyboards on the colored notecard, you'll go to the next scene in your script. Repeat this process using the same layout and form on each card, as well as matching the color of the card to whether or not the scene takes place inside/outside or day/night.

Following is an example of a traditional Breakdown Sheet.

SCENE #	PAGE COUNT:

SCENE NAME:		
INT / EXT:	D / N:	GOLDEN / BLUE HOUR:

Script Page:	Location Name:

Scene Description:

Cast	Extras	Wardrobe
	MU/Hair	
Special Effects	**Props**	**Vehicles**
Special Equipment	**Animals**	**Special Effects MU/Hair**
Visual Effects	**Other Notes**	

Here is an example of how I structure the layout of my notecards:

Scene #	(Filming Location)	(Filming Time)
		Cast
		Cast
	Description of scene	Cast
		Cast
		Cast
(SFX / VFX / SPECIALS)		(Vehicles / SPECIALS)

THE ARRANGEMENT

When you have every scene from your script documented onto the notecards, the next step is to separate them into piles based on shooting location or by the cast. If you have a movie star in your movie and that person is only available for a week, you must shoot all the scenes which include that person during that person's available time window. By sorting only the scenes that include the movie star, you'll be able to schedule appropriately and use your time most effectively during the time you have that person. If your entire cast is available for the complete duration of shooting, you will instead sort your notecards into stacks based on the shooting location.

Budget Side Note: The reason you do this is to save time and money. You do not want to pay people to be there when they don't have to be. Likewise, you don't have the time to run back and forth all over town day after day or your shoot will take twice as long to complete. That's twice as many meals to feed, twice as many days paid to talent, etc.

Put all the cards that take place at "the house" in one pile, all the cards which take place at "the restaurant" in another pile, and so on.

If you have a big house with multiple scenes taking place in the bedroom, and another set of scenes taking place in the kitchen, you might make the choice to consolidate the cards into smaller piles associated by the room inside the overall location. Once the bedroom has been wired and lit accordingly, and all the equipment assembled in the bedroom, it makes more sense to execute all the bedroom scenes before tearing down the lights and gear and moving into the kitchen. If you choose to film a scene in the bedroom, then move everything to the kitchen, then tear down all the equipment again and go back up to the bedroom, you'll be wasting a lot of time. My advice is to plan to film all the bedroom scenes and then move to the kitchen. If you agree, make smaller piles of cards based on rooms inside the house.

Here is an example of arranging notecards:

STEVE BALDERSON

THINK AHEAD

In all the years living in Los Angeles and taking meetings or having lunch with producers, certain actors, writers, or other friends not in the entertainment business, only two people have ever arrived at the meeting place on time. On one of those occasions, the other person was already there waiting for me when I arrived early. That was quite a shock and felt both exciting and intimidating. I am always on time or early. I prefer to be a little bit early so that I have time to walk around and explore.

A lot of people use traffic as the excuse, or something else which is not an abnormality, like the trouble of finding a parking space in a crowded metropolitan area. "Oh, getting here was an ordeal," they usually say as they rush towards me flustered and out of breath. (Again, an observation of chaos, panic and rushing to express business or productivity). The only thing that's true is that they failed to calculate and plan ahead to get there on time, or early.

If you don't know how long it takes to drive from A to B, you can easily access this data right from your phone or computer. If it takes 15 minutes to travel that distance, and you decide to stop somewhere in the middle, say, to pick up your laundry or mail a package, the length of time traveling from A to B will take even longer than originally expected. I would assume everyone knows this, but it's clearly not the case.

Perhaps 20 years ago when the traffic wasn't as bad, people could get from Hollywood to Santa Monica in 20 minutes. I don't know. Times have changed. It's important to adapt to the situation as it is, not how you'd like it to be.

I chuckle when I consider what might go through someone's mind when they wait until eight minutes prior to the confirmed meeting time before beginning the 15-minute drive. Do they think they will arrive on time? Do they know they will not? Are they making this choice on purpose to insult you or are they totally oblivious to it?

My hunch is that most people operate in a state of being oblivious to the world around them most of the time. But you won't need to. You'll be prepared to find out how long it takes to drive from A to B, and no matter what stops you take along the way, you'll add in time to account for those stops, and you'll arrive at your destination right on target.

Why it is important to schedule and plan ahead instead of just winging it? Planning can be a fun and enjoyable activity. A lot of artists dislike planning, but I see it as a very creative endeavor. It takes a lot of intuition, imagination and creativity to make a plan.

Scheduling and planning saves time, money and resources. Thinking ahead and being prepared keeps a person equipped with the resources they might need in any situation. Of course, there are some instances where people can practice misdirected planning. For instance, let's consider the survivalists living in underground bunkers planning for the end of the world or the apocalypse. Living amongst boxes packed full of canned goods, ammunition, and power generators will definitely come in handy if there is an apocalypse. But, since the apocalypse is likely not going to happen anytime soon, that's a bit like planning for a hurricane when you're filming on location in Nebraska or South Dakota. The survivalists are planning for things that have a 99% probability of not happening. They are not planning for all the things that could actually happen. Directed planning is important to remember so that you are prepared for whatever is likely to happen, or could happen, in your specific situation and circumstance.

DOCUMENTS

In the movie business, there are several varieties of schedules with various purposes.

The One-Liner Schedule is an abbreviated version of your shooting schedule. It looks like a horizontal stripboard. Each of your scenes are organized in the same order you will shoot them and separated by calendar days.

The Day out of Days Schedule is a chart that shows which days each actor is working. This document cannot be made until after your shooting schedule is complete. It's usually used to manage the budget of paying your actors and how to organize their working days.

Here is an example of a Day out of Days schedule.

	Month/Day	10/24	10/25	10/26	10/27	10/28	10/29	10/30	10/31	11/01
	Day of Week	Mon	Tue	Wed	Thu	Fri	Sat	Sun	Mon	Tue
	Shooting Day	1	2	3	4	5	6		7	8
1.	Carol		SW	W	W	W	W		W	W
2.	Brad	SW	W	W					W	W
3.	Billy		SW	W	W	W	W		W	W
4.	Frank				SW	W	W		W	W
5.	Father Earl								SW	W
6.	Young Billy									
7.	Jack									
8.	Desmond									
9.	Rudolpho									
10.	Vicki									
11.	Thaddeus	SW								
12.	Edmond	SW								
13.	Carl					SW	WF			
14.	Mave									
15.	Angry Man									
16.	Waitress	SWF								
17.	Teacher	SWF								
18.	Criminal								SWF	
19.	Old Lady								SWF	

Here is a traditional Shooting Schedule (also known as the one liner schedule). Notice the absence of actual filming time.

* * SHOOT MANSION * *					
Est call time 7:00AM on Set					
23	INT BEDROOM	D6	1/8 pgs	1, 3	MANSION
67	INT BEDROOM	D12	2/8 pgs	2, 3	MANSION
7	INT BEDROOM	D3	3 pgs	2, 3	MANSION
58	INT BEDROOM CLOSET	D61	1/8 pgs	1	MANSION
102	INT BEDROOM	D82	4/8 pgs	2	MANSION
* * MOVE TO KITCHEN * *					
11	INT KITCHEN	D12	1/8 pgs	1, 8, 9	Mansion
14	INT KITCHEN	D7	2 pgs	1, 8	Mansion
End Day #1 Tuesday, January 11, 2022 -- Total Pages: 6 1/8					
* * SHOOT JACKSON * *					
Est call time 7:00AM on Set					
45 pt 2	EXT ALLEY	D12	1/8 pgs	2, 3	3rd St Alley
47	EXT ALLEY	D12	2/8 pgs	2, 3	3rd St Alley
48	EXT ALLEY	D12	2/8 pgs	2, 3	3rd St Alley
End Day #2 Wednesday, January 12, 2022 -- Total Pages: 5/8					

CALL SHEETS

From this Shooting Schedule, call sheets are made.

Director		
Executive Producer		
Production Coordinator		
Basecamp		
Crew Park		
Tech Trucks		
BG Holding		
BG Parking		
Nearest Hospital:		

Call Sheet Title
Day 00 of 00

Shoot Date

Crew Call	
Shoot Call	
Breakfast	
Lunch	

Sc.	I/E	Setting/Description	D/N	Pages	8ths	Duration	Cast	Location	DD	Unit
					Test					
End of Day #00										

#	Character	Artist	SWF	PU	H/M/W	Block	Set Call	Special Instructions, Misc.

Transport Notes

Departmental Notes

Production			Hair			Production Office		
Director			Key Hair			Coordinator		
Assistant Directors			**Makeup**			Travel Coordinator		
1st AD			Key Makeup			Office P.A		
2nd AD			**Wardrobe**			**Accounting**		
Set PA			Costume Designer			Accountant		
Camera			**Art Department**			**Craft Service**		
DOP			Designer			Craft Server		
Camera Operator			Art Director			Catering		
1st AC			**Props**			**Transport**		
Sound			Props Master			Transport Captain		
Sound Mixer			Props Buyer			Head Driver		
Boom Op			**Set Decoration**			**Unit/Locations**		
Grip			Set Decorator			Location Manager		
Key Grip			Set Dresser			Locations P.A.		

INFLUENCES

Various considerations will affect your schedule:

Length of your script (feature vs. short)

Genre (special effects driven, period piece, road trip)

Shooting locations (your friend's house or an Italian villa on Lake Como, a sound stage or the actual restaurant)

Unions and Guilds

Length of Week (five-day weeks versus six-day weeks, versus no days off)

Budget Side Note: If people are working for a weekly rate, it won't matter if they are working five, six or seven days. However, which length of work week you decide upon will affect the length of your shoot, which will impact the budget.

Length of Day (12-hours, 14-hours, more?)

Budget Side Note: Overtime, safety concerns, etc., will impact your budget so consider this. It is often less expensive to add a few extra shooting days to your schedule than it is to pay overtime, emergency medical care, and so on.

STEVE BALDERSON

THE TIME IT TAKES TO SHOOT

When shooting an arrow, it isn't just about the act of watching the arrow fly through the air and hit the target. In order to do this activity, you must reverse the steps. First you will need to have an arrow. And to help the arrow, you will need to have a bow. The bow should probably fit your body size. If you acquire a bow that is made for a child, it might be awkward to use, and thus, influence how well the arrow makes it to your target. If the bow is too big, you might not get the tension needed to spring the arrow forward with enough force. You'll also need a target.

Attaching an actual shooting time to your scenes is one of the first elements which makes The Master Plan unique and radical. The next step is equally as important and often overlooked, or in most cases, totally disregarded.

We're going to operate with the notion that our schedule will be created in such a way that we will never exceed a 12-hour workday. But how in the world do we do this? We know how to count.

Let's start with 12 hours to work with. As that is our goal, think of it as our currency. Time equals money. It takes around one hour from each day's "call time" to get the actors ready, cameras and lights ready, and everything set and ready for the first scene.

So, let's subtract one hour. Now we have 11 hours remaining. Subtract another hour for lunch. Even if you plan for lunch to be 30 minutes long, lunch time starts when the last person is served or has gone through the line to get food. The last person to get their food usually happens about 25-30 minutes after you've called "lunch break." So, realistically, lunch break will take an hour. Now, we're down to 10 remaining hours. If you are able to overnight your equipment on location, it should only take about 30 minutes to tear down at the end of the day. This leaves nine and a half shooting hours available for each day.

If you have a location change which requires a "company move" during the day, you'll subtract another hour or so (depending on the size of the move). My advice is to limit the number of location changes on any given day. Sometimes it makes more productive sense to have a half day at one location and really take your time. Instead of feeling the dread of a long day or the risk of going into overtime and breaking past that dreadful 12-hour mark.

Let's move forward knowing you only have nine and a half

hours to film things. This allows for an effective way to properly schedule your shoot.

Take the notecards which have been previously arranged into piles by location. First, take the cards which refer to scenes to be filmed in the bedroom. Start by laying them out vertically in order by which they occur numerically. The first scene at the top, and then the next underneath. When you get finished with all the bedroom cards, count out the number of hours written on the upper right-hand corner. If the total is "11 hours" my advice is to take the bottom card (which reads "two hours") and move it to the next day. This gives you a solid day of nine filming hours, which should end up making your shoot day last 11 hours and 30 minutes.

If you are ambitious and find that you are running ahead of schedule, or if your crew doesn't mind having one day exceed 12 working hours, you might decide to include that final two-hour bedroom scene on that day after all. Another situation might be that you have permission to film in the bedroom for only one working day, which means you must complete the execution of all the bedroom scenes in the same day. To prevent working more than 12 hours, you might want to reevaluate the camera designs or shot lists which led to the filming time required for each bedroom scene. How might you and your DP re-design the shots to allow for easier execution and keep the active filming time in the bedroom to under nine and a half hours?

THE PAGE IS JUST A PAGE

Remember earlier when I mentioned that a scene in a script has a length of page associated with it? Such as the first bedroom scene taking up about half of the script page? Commonly, when doing the script breakdown, instead of writing down the hours or minutes required to execute and film the scene, people usually just make the note "1/2 page." Or "5/8 page" or "1/8 page" and so on.

If you aren't used to breaking down a script, learning to measure how long a scene is based on the length of the page might be confusing.

Historically, a script supervisor would put a ruler on each page and separate it into eighths.

On average, one page of a screenplay equals one minute of

screen time. This all depends on how much prose is used to describe the scene, or whether it's all dialogue and could change based on fast-paced or slow-paced delivery by actors. Basically, it is understood that a 90-page script will end up being a film that plays for something like 90 minutes.

Using those measurements, you could say that if a scene is 5/8ths of a page that scene will run just over 30 seconds on screen.

Traditionally, production personnel use the page lengths of a scene as a means of organizing the filming schedule. Often, people refer to organizing their shoots in the mindset they will shoot "six pages per day" or "we'll be lucky to film seven pages per day."

That practice, while customary in approach, is utterly inefficient.

A more effective way to plan your shooting day is to count the amount of time needed to execute the scene in question. You might have a car chase scene that is only half a page in length but will take five hours to execute. Likewise, you might have a two-page restaurant scene where the actors just sit there and talk to each other which might only take one hour to execute. Both of which might only make up about one minute of finished and edited screen time.

Forget about associating scenes with page lengths.

Forget about basing your shooting schedules around filming "pages" each day. You're filming cinematic scenes, not pages.

The only question to ask is: How long will it take to execute and film this scene?

Reminder: time equals money.

On a typical film shoot the First AD's job is to keep the cast and crew on schedule. This isn't easy or economical when you're basing your filming day around an arbitrary number of script page lengths.

Traditionally, at the end of every workday call sheets are distributed with the information detailing the next shooting day. In each call sheet there is the following information:

Cast and crew call times (what time to arrive for work).

The address of the location where filming will take place (with parking information).

The address for the nearest hospital with an emergency room.

What scenes will be filmed (and how many pages in length each has).

Which actors appear in which scenes (and the time they need to arrive in the makeup chair to prepare).

Contact names and numbers (the director, producer, first assistant director, and the production manager).

General or special notes (should there be any pyrotechnics or explosions for example).

Walkie-talkie channel assignments for each department.

All that information is valuable and should be included somewhere on your daily call sheets. But there is an important omission which needs to be added. With exception to the call times for crew and when an actor needs to arrive on set, the most important element is missing:

Time.

If call time is 6am and it is 1:30pm there is no way to know where you are in the progress of the day. If it's after lunch and you're in the middle of a scene, how can you adequately evaluate whether you're staying on schedule or falling behind? There isn't any way to know. It might be obvious you are behind if you are supposed to execute six pages today and you've been on set for ten hours and have so far only managed to execute two. Operating in a traditional way makes it all a blur and before you know it, you're deep into overtime with a fatigued and cantankerous crew working their 14th hour.

My first two films were produced using this traditional process. And on those two features we certainly experienced several 14-hour days. At the time I didn't know whether that was simply the way it was, or if the slow pace and lack of organization was my fault. I started to wonder if there was anything I could do which might help make filming more efficient.

It came to me when I was in pre-production for my third feature film. I examined the earlier experiences and asked what happened to cause the long hours. I wanted to learn and to find out! After all, it was in my best interest.

I had been totally prepared in both cases with detailed shot lists and storyboards explaining how we'd execute each scene. There seemed to constantly be a state of forward motion. No one seemed to be lazily lounging around (although there were a number of crew positions filled by people I later learned we didn't need to have on set). If none of that caused the long hours, what did? What caused the long days?

It was quite simple—focusing on the page length and not thinking about the clock!

THE ACCIDENTAL PLANNER

I operate with a daily routine that pretty much runs like clockwork each day of the week. I get up at roughly the same time each day without the need of an alarm. I am always on time or early for an appointment. I take into consideration traffic time, travel time, parking time, and walking time. Each activity in my day is done with military precision. My grandfather was in the military, and I was raised with a daily structure that might stem from that (and the way my mother was raised). Or it's in my DNA. Who knows.

I have always preferred to use a daily calendar which is reminiscent of the big planning books used by hair salons in the 1990s to schedule their appointments. In it I record my meetings, tasks, and so on. The smart phone calendar has never worked for me. It's visually uninteresting and not as easy to use. Plus, sometimes the digital reminders I schedule don't actually pop up and remind me to do anything.

Regardless of publisher, my ideal daily planner is separated by increments of 15 minutes. Each day is arranged in a vertical column so that when opened flat, Monday through Wednesday is on the left page, and Thursday through Sunday is on the right. Each day has horizontal lines running through them beginning at 6:00am and charting every 15 minutes until 10:00pm.

When I was in pre-production on my third feature, I had decided I would be my own cinematographer. I thought maybe if I were in charge of the crew, things would move along more efficiently. They did. But I learned it wasn't that I was the director and the DP at the same time that made a difference. What mattered was the way I went about planning the schedule for the shoot.

It was the birth of The Master Plan.

I thought, well, if I'm going to direct and be the DP and also be the cameraman, I need to be super ready. Beyond prepared. More organized than I had ever been. We had a sufficient budget, but it was limited. There were not endless financial resources. It was my responsibility to make every dollar and minute count.

Instinctively, I knew how long it would take me to film and execute each scene. I only had myself to answer to. If I were going to have the crew set up lights, I knew where they were to be placed and how long that might take. I knew how long it would take to drive to the location, how long it would take to set everything up, the number of shots in the scene, and how long each shot would take to shoot.

I remembered those late hours that ran deep into the night on my previous two features. I just made the conscious decision that there was no reason to have horrendously long hours in my life. I hated filming all night long. I value sleep and taking care of my mental wellbeing. If a "night" scene takes place inside, I decided we would film it during the day. The only scenes that need to be filmed at night are scenes that happen outside at night. I decided to split it up by maybe doing one night scene or shot each evening instead of spending all night long filming all of them at once.

In addition to sleep, I value a strong work ethic and good nutrition. Instead of always waiting until six hours into the shoot from whatever call time happened to be, we would eat lunch at lunch time. Even if it were only three hours into the shoot day. Likewise, we would wrap at a reasonable hour in order to appreciate a cast and crew happy hour and dinner each night.

If having all that seems impossible to you, let me assure you this is how I've structured and scheduled every feature since that third shoot of mine. And there have been 18 more at the time of this writing.

I decided to use my daily planner as a template. The following is an example of how I structured the first day.

Call time at 7am.

That meant first shot off at 8am.

If we were to shoot Scene One at 8am and it required 90 minutes to execute, I would assign Scene Two to begin filming at 9:30am.

Scene Two was estimated to take one hour to execute.

That led to Scene Three, with another 90-minute execution, which would begin at 10:30am and lead us to lunch break at High Noon.

Then at 1:00pm we would return from lunch and shoot Scene Four.

And so on until 6:00pm when we planned to wrap for the day.

I used that basic structure for each day of the shoot. Because I knew myself, my pace and what I wanted for each scene, I was confident I'd remain pretty much on schedule throughout the shoot. I didn't know that for certain, my hunch was simply a guess at that point.

I used a Microsoft Word document to build a template like the layout of my ideal daily planner—using clock time which was divided into 15-minute intervals. Then I took the useful information from a traditional call sheet and incorporated it into my document. I assigned actual times on the clock to each moment of the day. Each scene was attached to clock time. No page lengths would ever be referred to again. After all, the only thing that matters is how long something will take to execute. Not how long it measures in writing.

When I completed the document, I titled it jokingly, The Master

Plan.

I gave copies of The Master Plan to each person on the cast and crew. By having their own copies, it would help them know on any given day, at any time during the day, whether we were on schedule, ahead of schedule, or falling behind. All you had to do is look at the time on the clock and then glance at The Master Plan. If it's 2:30pm and we were supposed to be done with this scene at 2pm, we're behind. If it's 4:15pm and we're ready to start the next scene, which was scheduled to start at 4:45pm, we're already 30 minutes ahead of schedule.

Another useful quality about The Master Plan is that the way it is presented shows all the 15-minute intervals throughout the day. If Scene Six has a three-hour execution, it will visually take up a large portion of the page for the schedule that day. The visual depiction communicates a scene taking longer or shorter than others to execute. Knowing what the day looked like visually kept everyone else as prepared as I was.

Before finalizing The Master Plan, I also consulted with the makeup department. If Hillary's makeup and hair takes 30 minutes to finish, and I want her on set camera-ready at 3pm, Hillary had better be in the makeup seat no later than 2:30pm. And knowing actors as I do, we ought to consider giving Hillary a call time of 2pm (or earlier) so that no one is waiting on her to get into that makeup seat.

Obstacles arise and challenges occur no matter how prepared

and organized you are. That's just how life goes. There were days we were running behind. And there were days we were ahead of schedule. In my experience in all the feature films which followed my first two, only once did a working day exceed my 12-hour promise. For that I apologized profusely. To make up for it, I hired a massage therapist to come to set and work on people periodically throughout the day—anyone who wanted one.

The casts and crews who have worked in productions using The Master Plan can attest to experiencing, on average, 10-hour workdays. There are even a couple films where everyone experienced a six-hour workday.

If this sounds too good to be true just ask people I've worked with. Try it out for yourself and find out. Experience it.

It works. It saves time. It saves money.

COMMUNICATION

Almost every person in our culture is operating with inadequate, if not poor communication skills—even when they think they are good communicators.

I always thought I was a good communicator until I learned the DNA of communication. That's when a lightbulb went off and really changed how effective my communication could be. It changed every interaction I've had since.

One of the things to understand is that the meaning of communication isn't what you say – it's what the other person hears. If I'm speaking English and the other person only speaks Swedish, it's likely that no matter how clearly I enunciate, it won't do any good. I might even try speaking louder in order for the other person to understand me. Many American tourists practice this when travelling abroad in countries where they speak in languages other than English. (I used to think that was a total cliché, but I've witnessed it hundreds of times in actual situations).

The DNA of communication is made up of the following:

7% Words—predicates, key words, common experiences & associations and content (are the words vague and "big picture" or specific and detailed?)

38% Tonality—tone (pitch, high/low), tempo (speed, fast/slow), timbre (quality, crisp/raspy), volume (loudness)

55% Physiology—posture, facial expression and blinking, gesture, breathing

This means that 93% of meaningful communication is unconscious. Furthermore, if only 7% of communication is made up of words, it makes your choice of words incredibly important.

Another aspect to consider is how each person's mind processes information. The main three ways are Visually, Auditorily and Kinesthetically. I'm predominately a visual person. When my mind takes in new information it arrives there in full understanding as an image. Then, my mind translates that image into words and sounds. Only after the translation do those images transform out of my mouth as words and sounds.

Many actors I know process information auditorily. Their minds take in sound before being able to translate those sounds into images and meaning. Many of the auditory people I know tend to discuss and describe things using sounds and words related to sounds. That's because it is how they best understand. The difficulty comes when that auditory person is talking to a visually-minded processor. I have a friend who processes auditorily. She won't send me an email when she has an idea, and instead calls me on the phone. By the end of the call, I have retained almost nothing of the conversation since I process visually, not auditorily. I've learned to ask her to send me an email of her thoughts after the call so I can make sure I got it all. That usually works!

Lastly, a kinesthetically minded person takes in information primarily based on the feeling. This group is very rare. Usually, human beings process situations and experiences either visually or auditorily.

Now that you know this, you can understand that each person on the planet speaks an individual language based on how they process information. Coupled with their own set of life's experiences. How they were raised, in what culture, in what environment, and so on.

NOTE: More can be found in the "Bonus" chapter on Communication in the Appendix.

In a field dominated by people who process visually, The Master Plan clearly communicates a greater amount of information than the traditional strips or call sheets.

Going back to the film I directed for Mark Cuban. On that shoot, because The Master Plan was totally new to everyone but me, my ADs printed the traditional call sheets at the end of every day just like they are used to. That was totally fine with me. I understand that traditional call sheets are the language they are used to and the language they speak. I instructed them to print The Master Plan on the reverse side. That way, each person could find out which format appealed to them the most.

Many repetitive questions asked of me on set came with my answer in the form of a question, "What does it say on The Master Plan?" Upon consulting The Master Plan, almost always they would find their answer. Soon, there were hardly any distracting questions for me to respond to.

Halfway into that shoot I asked my First AD (the awesome Kevin Huie) to begin passing call sheets out to the cast and crew with The Master Plan side facing up. As a way to communicate that The Master Plan side was primary. By doing so, the cast and crew could become more and more familiar with it, and if a person ever got confused, they could flip the sheet over and find the archaic call sheet they were used to on the back.

Here are some excerpts from The Master Plan as used on several of my feature films.

THE MASTER PLAN

WEDNESDAY 4 AUGUST 2021
Sunrise 6:06 AM, Sunset 7:51 PM

LOCATION: W Jefferson Blvd, 90016 PARKING: Street, read signs	**WEATHER** Report.
NEAREST EMERGENCY ROOM Kaiser Hospital: 6041 Cadillac Ave Hospital West Tower, Los Angeles, CA 90034	**HISTORY** 1693 – Celebratory date for Dom Perignon's invention of Champagne

TIME	SCENE			WHO / WHERE
9:30				
9:45			Time obscure: No source of Day or Night	
10:00			**CAST & CREW CALL @ BERT'S**	
10:15			How to avoid being late: always leave earlier	
10:30	33-37	B	**RITUAL:** Wide guys	1,2,4,5,6,7,8,9,10,11,12,13,14
10:45			CU each guy tension	15
11:00			On Nigel	
11:15			On Amira	
11:30	39-42	B	On Amira / KevCam on Eddie also	1,2,3,13,14,15
11:45			On Marcus dies / INS CU syringe SFX	Change to F clothes
12:00	105-107	F	**RITUAL:** Wide guys	1,2,4,5,6,7,8,9,10,11,15,18
12:15			CU each guy tension	JAKE: Prep Felix throat slit
12:30			On Nigel	
12:45			On Amira	
13:00 – 1			**LUNCH BREAK**	Larchmont wine & cheese deli
13:15				
13:30				
13:45			Lay down tarp?	
14:00 – 2	108B	F	Single on Felix dies SFX	1,11
14:15				
14:30			Change clothes	
14:45	120-122	G	Wide on guys, CU Nigel/Amira	1,2,4,5,6,7,8,9
15:00 – 3			Change clothes	
15:15	134-136	H	**RITUAL:** Time's up	1,2,4,5,6,7,8,9
15:30	137-138	H	On Beaux	1,2,3,9,15,18
15:45			On Amira	
16:00 – 4			INS mirror swish pan	
16:15			On Beaux SFX cut face and strangle	
16:30			On Amira	
16:45			INS she grabs shard of mirror	
17:00 – 5			INS she stabs his neck SFX he dies	
17:15	139-140	H	**STAGED CRYING:** on Amira	1,2,3,14,15
17:30			On Nigel	
17:45			KevCam: on Eddie	
18:00 – 6	156	H	**RITUAL:** Wide on guys, CU each?	1,2,4,5,6,7
18:15			On Nigel/Amira	
18:30			Change to L clothes	
18:45	196-198	L	**RITUAL:** On Nigel pan D'M/Amir fight	1,2,3,5,7,14
19:00 – 7			Angle two fight	
19:15			On Eddie / Amira	
19:30			On Amir getting shot, his body	
19:45	208	L	On Amira, On D'Marcus	
20:00 – 8			Two shot	
20:30			**WRAP – CAN STAGE OVERNIGHT**	
20:45				

"What a caterpillar calls the end of the world we call a butterfly."
Eckhart Tolle

73

MONDAY 14 OCTOBER
Sunrise: 6:55 AM – Sunset 6:03 PM

CONTACTS:	NEAREST HOSPITAL (32 miles)
Steve Balderson	Maine Medical Center ER (Portland)
Clark Balderson	
Hanuman Brown	**WEATHER**
Nathanael Lentz	High: 61°F – Low: 38°F
Jake Jackson	Partly Cloudy, Precip 10%
Elizabeth Spear	

Time	Sc	Description	CAST
11:00		SPEND MORNING STAGING THE SET	CAST
11:15			
11:30			
11:45			
12:00		**LUNCH** at Home Base:	
12:15		, Limerick, ME 04048	
12:30			
12:45			
13:00 – 1		**CALL @ MANSION**	Limerick, 04048
13:15		Crew set up	
13:30			
13:45	Sc 15	Various Rooms	
14:00 – 2			
14:15	Sc 101	Healthy House, various rooms	
14:30			
14:45			
15:00 – 3		Go out to wild house and areas	
15:15	Sc 36	Exterior various	
15:30			
15:45	Various	Landscapes on stix and drone	
16:00 – 4			(Oliver get ready for sc 42 INS)
16:15			
16:30	INS 42	Oliver's BIKE RIDE – DRONE	Oliver
16:45			
17:00 – 5			
17:15			
17:30			
17:45			
18:00 – 6		Move to trees	
18:15	Sc 6	The trees – DRONE	
18:30			
18:45			
19:00 – 7		**WRAP**	
19:10		Drive to Home base for happy hour	* Oliver's trench coat or hoodie
19:30			for Doppelganger sc tomorrow
19:45			
20:00 – 8		**DINNER** at Home Base	
20:10		Limerick, ME 04048	* Eliza lands 11pm AA1289
20:30			Tonight, rental car to Limerick
20:45			

THE MASTER PLAN

Sunrise: 6:59 AM – Sunset: 5:58 PM

CONTACTS:	NEAREST HOSPITAL (32 miles)
Steve Balderson	Maine Medical Center ER (Portland)
Clark Balderson	
Hanuman Brown-Eagle	WEATHER
Nathanael Lentz	High: 54°F – Low: 36°F
Jake Jackson	AM Showers, Precip 40%
Elizabeth Spear	

Time	Scene	Description	Cast
8:15			
8:30		**CALL @ MANSION**	Limerick, 04048
8:45		Crew set up / cast make-up ready	
9:00			
9:15			
9:30	35	BEDROOM – Another universe, the "guides"	Oliver & Evelyn
9:45		And "5 days left"	
10:00			
10:15			
10:30			
10:45			
11:00			
11:15			
11:30			
11:45			
12:00		**LUNCH** at Home Base	
12:15		Limerick, ME 04048	
12:30			
12:45			
13:00 – 1	37	BEDROOM – the feather	Oliver & Evelyn
13:15			
13:30	41	KITCHEN – second coffee cup, sex scene	Oliver & Evelyn
13:45			
14:00 – 2			
14:15			
14:30	42	STUDIO – Heaven, pills, the Unknown	Oliver & Evelyn
14:45			
15:00 – 3			
15:15			
15:30			
15:45			
16:00 – 4			
16:15			
16:30			
16:45			
17:00 – 5	43pt1	Oliver wakes, back in his chair after bike ride	Oliver, Evelyn
17:15			
17:30			
17:45			
18:00 – 6		**WRAP**	
18:15			
18:30		Go to Home Base for Happy Hour	
18:45			
19:00 – 7		**DINNER** at Home Base	
19:10		Limerick, ME 04048	
19:30			
19:45			

THURS, SEPTEMBER 22

		"Call" means camera ready (M/U, hair, costume done)	CREW today:
Actors today:			SB (director)
ADEELA		BIG GUY (8 PM)	MPage (asst)
MICK			A1 (sound / cam2)
JACK			NO TOM
			James Merchant

Props: "Bonnie" video, pendent, Big Guy's rifle

14:00 – 2			
14:15			
14:30			
14:45			
15:00 – 3		CALL = **MEET IN ROOM**	
15:15		District or Circle Line to Victoria	
15:30		Victoria Line to Oxford Circus	
15:45			
16:00 – 4	60/61	Street post kidnapping	AMJ
16:15		(LOCATION: Portland or Wardour Mews)	
16:30			
16:45			
17:00 – 5			
17:15			
17:30	62	Tiny Alleyway – undies/pendent	AMJ
17:45		(LOCATION: Portland or Wardour Mews)	
18:00 – 6			
18:15			
18:30		Dinner at: Breakfast Club: 33 D'Arblay St, W1F 8	
18:45			
19:00 – 7		(There's an EAT on Soho Sq)	
19:15		(Inamo: 134-136 Wardour St, W1F 8ZP)	
19:30		Central line to Lancaster Gate	
19:45			
20:00 – 8	64	Street on the move to find computer	AMJ
20:15		(LOCATION 203-211 Sussex Gardens)	
20:30	65	Townhome	AMJ, Big Guy
20:45		(LOCATION: 235 Sussex Gardens)	
21:00 – 9			
21:15			
21:30	66	Street post Big Guy	AMJ
21:45		(LOCATION: Talbot Square)	
22:00 – 10		**WRAP**	
22:15		Walk to Paddington, Circle Line back to SJP	
22:30			
22:45			
23:00 – 11			
23:15			
23:30			

Starina leaves LAX on Virgin Atlantic Flight 8 at 5:35 PM her time

YOUR MASTER PLAN

To make your Master Plan you'll need to create a template (or copy the one I came up with using Microsoft Word). I use Word because that's where I built it first, so I have blank templates ready to use at any moment.

One of my ADs made a template in Excel because that program works best for her. So long as the daily schedule is broken down into 15-minute intervals of clock time and reflects the actual filming time for each scene (not the page length of the scene as it relates to the script), the program you use to create the Master Plan is irrelevant.

Another important thing to take into consideration are bathroom breaks, set-up times, and any kind of company move during the day. Even if it's a move from the second floor of the mansion down to the first floor, there will be time spent in doing that move. Make a conscious effort to plan for it. Even if you have crew members pre-lighting and setting up downstairs while everyone else is upstairs filming, there will still be at least 15-minutes spent getting people to simply walk their bodies down the staircase once the last upstairs shot is in the can. Even if you wish they would all walk down together at the same time, they won't.

If it takes the make-up and hair person 30 minutes to park, get their gear on set, and prepare their station for an actor, and another 30 minutes before that actor is ready, that's fine. Plan for it.

Planning ahead is one of the keys to building a successful Master Plan. If you wait until later, or forget something, it might shave off enough clock time so much so, that had you thought about it, you might have scheduled that day in a totally different way.

It's important once you've made a rough version of your Master Plan to share it with your DP. Your DP will be thinking about time and movement from a perspective that might inform what you need to change or add. Also show your First AD and any other Production Department Head who might be helpful with contributing to the Master Plan. Once you have everyone's input, you can add things that need to be added, make any other corrections, and then you'll have your final Master Plan.

Taking responsibility is key.

If you are lazy and don't want the responsibility of making your

Master Plan, you need to communicate as carefully and specifically as possible to whomever is making your Master Plan for you. Remember when speaking to this person: it isn't the words you use—it's what that other person hears.

Time management is key.

If you have a reluctance to plan ahead, a history of running late or forgetting appointments, it won't be easy to swiftly move into having a structure in which time becomes important for you. That's okay. Have someone else make your Master Plan and then hire another person to keep you on schedule.

Developing a relationship with time where you can be punctual, thoughtful, with insight when it comes to planning ahead, takes... well... time. It doesn't happen overnight. It takes effort to change a habit. Even though it might take four weeks to break an old habit, it might only take two weeks to develop a new habit. My advice is to think about it as a totally new habit. That way the goal might be easier to reach.

Turn the page for a basic template to make your Master Plan.

STEVE BALDERSON

DAY DATE MONTH
Sunrise: 6:57 AM – Sunset: 6:02 PM

CONTACTS:	NEAREST HOSPITAL (? miles)
Producer (phone) First AD (phone)	Address
	WEATHER
(Whomever you want to list, knowing that the entire cast and crew will see phone #s in this document)	High: 58°F – Low: 37°F Sunshine, Precip 5%

Time	Sc	Description	Cast/Address
8:30			
8:45			
9:00		**CALL @ LOCATION**	Address
9:15		Set up	
9:30			
9:45			
10:00	Sc #	Scene title, description	CAST in this scene
10:15			
10:30			
10:45			
11:00			
11:15			
11:30			
11:45			
12:00		**LUNCH** on set	
12:15			
12:30			
12:45			
13:00 – 1	Sc #	Scene title, description	CAST in this scene
13:15			
13:30			
13:45			
14:00 – 2			
14:15			
14:30			
14:45			
15:00 – 3			
15:15			
15:30			
15:45			
16:00 – 4			
16:15			
16:30			
16:45			
17:00 – 5			
17:15			
17:30			
17:45			
18:00 – 6		**WRAP**	
18:15		Tear down, clears location	
18:30			
18:45			
19:00 – 7		**GONE**	
19:10			
19:30			

Fun quote, inspiring aspiration, or weird fact "on this date in history" etc.

SCHEDULING FOR PLAN B

In planning ahead, you must consider solutions to potential conflicts before the conflicts occur. This way, if a conflict or challenge does occur, you will know the steps to take.

Chaos is almost always avoidable.

Chaos comes when you haven't planned ahead.

You don't have to have a contingency plan for every possible scenario. Just the likely-to-happen or possible ones. If the forecast calls for a chance of rain and you are to be filming outside, you might want to plan for rain even if it doesn't rain. If it rains, you'll be prepared to act accordingly. If it doesn't rain, no worries. At least you were prepared. Praying and hoping it doesn't rain won't prepare you for what to do if it ends up raining.

Once I was directing for a production which was filming at night in a night club. When the shoot was wrapped, we began the process of packing up equipment and gear. I wanted to be helpful, so I went to turn on the house lights so that the crew could see what they were doing. I couldn't find the switch. I asked the producer if she knew where the switch was located. She didn't and went to find the owner.

Eventually, I was informed that the house lights were somehow tied to the house lights in the bar downstairs. If they were turned on, the house lights in the bar would go on and the bar patrons would leave. The owner of the location didn't want people to leave, so he would not allow us to turn on the lights.

I was forced to inform my crew they would be packing up their gear in the dark. The producer wasn't fazed with the safety concerns of working in the dark, let alone the potential for accidentally forgetting to pack up any gear or equipment that had been rented because we couldn't see it. The owner didn't seem to care if we damaged the property moving large c-stands and other heavy equipment while navigating the space and hallways on our way outside.

Usually, when filming outside at night, especially if you're in a field, it is common for people to bring flashlights or headlamps to wear, so that when it's time to turn off the big lights used for filming and pack up the gear, there is a light source.

Yes, on this occasion it was a night shoot. A night shoot happening inside a location with operational electricity. In 25 years, I've never experienced (or even heard of) a situation where we weren't allowed to turn on the lights once we were finished. This was a first. It was also the first time that a production I was working on had no flashlights or headlamps, or any other means to see things in the dark.

Now I know to ask for the ability to turn on the lights at locations in the future. Even though it seems ludicrous and ridiculous to ask. Whenever I do eventually ask this, I imagine whomever the producer is wondering if I'm micro-managing a little too far. I also imagine whomever the location owner ends up being, to roll their eyes and laugh at me while asking, with a sound of being offended, "Why on earth would you think I wouldn't let you turn on the lights so you could see what you're doing? What kind of person do you think I am?"

WHAT WILL YOU DO IF...?

Planning ahead and having a back-up plan when necessary is always a good practice.

Imagine how your schedule might change, or what solution you will implement if one of the following occurs during your shoot. What will you do? How will you handle it? How will you make the decisions needed to reach your desired outcome if one of these things happens?

Weather

Always look at the forecast. You'll need to have more drinking water on hand for hot days than you would normally. Tents to protect people from the sun if you're outside. Space heaters for freezing temperatures. Rain gear, tents, umbrellas, electrolyte powder, sunscreen, bug repellant, coolers with bags of ice, hand warmers, and on and on.

Destruction of a location

Say you're planning to film all day in a big red barn. First, find out if there's electricity in the barn. If there isn't, you'll need a generator or power to pull electricity from somewhere.

What if, on the day of the shoot, you arrive on set only to find out that the big red barn burned to the ground last night. Complaining and being shocked won't build back the barn. You'll need to quickly move to a different location. Or, if you've rented too many generators, porta-potties, and tents which are arriving at the location any minute now, and you can't move, you'll need to find a way to shoot the same scene outside in the field nearby where the barn used to be.

What if one of the crew people damage a wall? Do you have a contingency plan in place to pay the owner? All the proper insurance?

Injury of a cast or crew member

What if someone falls down the stairs, gets a concussion from a falling light, or worse? What if you're going to have actual guns as props instead of rubber ones?

I do want to take this moment to tell you that there is no reason whatsoever an actual real gun EVER needs to be on set. The rubber ones look just like the real ones. Computer generated effects are incredible now and they can make the smoke and fire in post. No one will ever know it wasn't a real gun. The danger of having a real gun on set, and the destruction they can cause, is far more detrimental and costly than renting a good realistic totally fake gun and doing all the visual effects work in post. Trust me. There is NEVER any reason whatsoever to have a real gun on set.

Illness

People catch colds. Hopefully, no one on your crew will suffer a significant illness in the middle of your shoot. But if they did, and you had to replace them, what would you do? What if it was your leading actor? Are you flexible? Can you move around scenes so that you can continue to work for a few days while the actor recuperates and becomes well enough to resume working?

Global Pandemic

Right?

WORST CASE SCENARIO

Obviously, we aren't psychic fortune tellers. We can't predict everything that might or will or could happen. We can, however, from past experience, ponder all the things that have happened and are likely or might happen in the future. There is likely not to be a hurricane in Nebraska anytime soon. If there is a hurricane while you're filming in Nebraska, which would need to extend all the way to the Gulf of Mexico or either ocean, you'll have a lot more catastrophic things to worry about than whether your production will continue.

Imagining the worst-case scenarios and finding solutions for them before they ever happen isn't being anxious or a worrywart. It's the logical thing to do when you are dealing with a period of time where you'll be responsible for the health and safety of a group of people. It is your responsibility to maintain their wellbeing and the cost associated with keeping them safe, well-fed, with a nice bed to sleep in, reliable transportation, and the resources and materials needed to do their jobs.

MANAGEMENT

Who's in charge of the schedule? Ultimately, YOU are responsible, no matter which job title you have. Every person is responsible for sticking to the schedule and being productive. It is the DP's job to make sure the crew is accomplishing tasks at the speed by which things have been planned. It's the make-up person's job to make sure faces and hairdos are done by the time they need to be done. It's the director's job to make sure the scenes are being captured and all the shots are filmed. It's the producer's job to make sure all the production elements are in place to keep the schedule on track. Failure by anyone in any department to stick to the Master Plan will upset or offset everyone else.

It is also a great idea to make sure you have a very well organized and thorough Manager or Management Person. One person whose only responsibility is communicating the time at hand and what guidance and help is needed to continue remaining on schedule.

Typically, this person is the 1ST AD (First Assistant Director). But it doesn't have to be the 1ST AD. This person could be someone else with a job title like UPM (Unit Product Manager), PM (Production Manager), LP (Line Producer), or even a PA (Production Assistant). Whomever this person is needs to have a full understanding of what is required to keep things on track from one hour to another and one to day to the next. Usually, a Line Producer manages the production elements from the "office" side of things. On independent shoots, a Line Producer wears more hats.

ENHANCING PRODUCTIVITY

Changing locations eats up a lot of time even if the other location is across the street. Half of your production day can be impacted by a "company move." My advice is to limit any chance at changing locations in the middle of your day unless it is to only prepare the next location for shooting the following day. The smaller the crew size, the easier it will be, but it will still take hours. If you must do a production move from one location to another in the same day, all you have to do is adequately plan for it.

Consider "tearing down time" where your crew will be clearing out their equipment from the first location and storing it back into the vehicles they arrived in. If you have new and different sized vehicles for departure, you'll need to find a way to fit all the gear that needs to be moved into these new vehicles ahead of time. Add up the amount of "set up time" you have in the new location, which should be the same you had in the previous location plus half more. Getting used to a new location takes a little longer than one you're already familiar with shooting in. Factor in driving time and multiply that by two or three. Undoubtedly someone will get lost, not know where to park, possibly get a flat tire, and so on.

DAYS OFF

It is customary that a production has either a five-day or six-day work week. Depending on the circumstances this can be different for each production. Once, I directed a feature film that didn't have any days off. We filmed every day for several weeks. Of course, I had my Master Plan in effect, so we never had a 12-hour workday, had plenty of good food and good sleep, and several half days.

For that film in particular we were on location deep in the middle of rural Maine nowhere near anything. There was absolutely nothing to do even if you wanted to do something. It was several hours drive to the nearest decent sized town, and an hour or so more to the nearest city. Before making the decision we would have no days off, I asked the crew if they would mind. I asked them what they would normally want. They said that normally they needed the days off to rest because they were being worked to the bone long hours and without respect to turnaround time. Having worked for me in the past, they knew they would have plenty of rest, good food, and respect. So, they agreed to work straight through without taking a day off and preferred it. Everyone was excited to get out of there and back to the city. No one wanted to take a day off because it would extend the date of evacuation.

Normally, you'd want to give your crew a day off now and then so they can do laundry and keep up to date on their bills or other lifestyle needs. But if you're working nonunion, there is no set rule for how it must be done. You can make your own standards. My advice is to always consider the other person. Do you want to work 14-hour days every day without a day off? I don't. So, I assume the people I'm working with don't want to either. Do you want to finally get to bed at 1:00am and have to wake back up at 5:00am in order to be on set by 6:00am? Me neither.

TURNAROUNDS

It is standard that there is a full 12 hours between the end of one production day to the start of the next. If you wrap and get done at 10:00pm, you must not have a call time the next day at 8:00am. The earliest ought to be 10:00am. This is what is called the "12-

hour Turnaround." Even for nonunion crews this is standard. Some people will put it in their contracts that if you do not give them an adequate turnaround time that overtime takes affect and adequate compensation be made.

Usually, call sheets are made at the end of every production day because during the day one realizes that you will wrap later than you'd hoped. And to give everyone a solid 12-hour turnaround means that you have to change the call times for everyone the next day. Very quickly things can get backlogged and lost due to poor planning.

When using the Master Plan, you might not need to do any of that. When I lock the Master Plan before a shoot, it's locked and adhered to. Each of the wrap times are either followed as scheduled or we're running ahead of schedule and wrap early. Never have I had a change in the call times for what was originally accounted and planned for. Thus, there have been a number of feature films I directed where I didn't even hire a 1ST AD to help me because there was otherwise nothing for them to do.

MEALTIMES

It is standard and ruled by law in some places that meals are served every six hours. The crew is not required to work six hours after having finished a meal unless there is another meal break.

It is also standard that if your lunch break is 30 minutes long, that those 30 minutes start only after the last person in line gets their food. Knowing that, if it takes 15 minutes for everyone to pick up their lunch boxes or go through the buffet table, your "30 minute" lunch break will actually be 45 minutes, so my advice is to always schedule an hour for a "30 minute" lunch break.

I dislike eating at weird hours. Therefore, I prefer to schedule lunch around lunchtime, dinner around dinner time, and so on. I still factor in the solid six-hour rule between meals, but sometimes I schedule the first meal only a couple hours after we've started. If we have a 9:00am call time, just because you must feed everyone every six hours doesn't mean you have to WAIT six hours. You can easily plan for lunch to happen at 12 noon or 1:00pm even if you have a 9:00am call time.

Once, I directed a feature film on location in London. On the first day of shooting, we worked for about two hours before taking our lunch break. People on the cast and crew made jokes and poked fun at me for planning the entire filming process around meals. It was true. I had. And they loved it.

OTHER FACTORS

Planning the production of a narrative feature film requires more work than planning to shoot a short film, but depending upon how you're shooting the short film, it might not.

If you are in the mindset of shooting nonstop (regardless how many days), you have one preparation period, one period of gathering rentals and equipment, one period where you're responsible for everyone on set, and one moment where you're returning the rented equipment. That's it.

If you decide to film your project on the weekends, or in spurts here and there, you will have more work to do than you would if you were just shooting it straight through. For each of those weekends, you will still have one preparation period, one period of gathering rentals and equipment, one period where you're responsible for everyone on set, and yet another moment where you're returning the rented equipment.

If you plan to shoot over four different weekends, you will do all of those things every single weekend. You will have eight trips back and forth gathering and returning rented equipment. Eight times you have to load up your car and unload it. Eight separate times you must plan ahead mealtimes and what to feed the crew. Do you really want to waste all that time driving back and forth, and the energy it takes to live that way? Perhaps you do. I don't. I've learned that working in a structure like that isn't as productive as just shooting straight through. There's nothing wrong with choosing that structure. Just be aware you're making that decision. You might find that it is far less time consuming (and less expensive) to just shoot straight through.

MORE MONEY

Having more money doesn't mean you'll have more resources; it just means you'll have more money. Having a lot of money doesn't guarantee your project will look good nor that anyone will want to watch it. It just means you'll have more money.

I have a very wealthy friend who has impeccable taste. What's so remarkable and admirable is that her taste isn't necessarily expensive. She simply has impeccable taste. When she was designing the interior of her new home, which was being totally gutted and remodeled, there were elements which were constructed out of plywood and recycled corrugated transparent plastic. Which, when combined with the aesthetic of the entire house, gives the interior a million-dollar look for a tiny fraction of the price.

Knowing that she spent next to nothing while living with the resources to spend as much as she wanted to, is the admirable part. This is how I approach filmmaking. My film FIRECRACKER looks like it cost a million dollars. It didn't. We spent significantly less than half that.

I have another friend who bought a restaurant and invested an enormous amount of money in the remodel, and in the end, it looked like he spent about $29.95. It was just awfully designed. The lighting was terrible and the experience being in that environment was dreadful. Money can't buy you taste and aesthetic awareness. It's a skillset, combining talent and creativity.

CREATING WITH RESTRAINTS

Whether the restraints are cash, your filming locations, the actors you've cast or whatever the cause, creating within limitations can be exciting. Having a dollar doesn't mean you have to spend it. First, try and find a way to get what you need without spending it. Think creatively.

Is there another way to acquire that thing you want or need?

Are you truly needing it, or do you just want it?

How would having this thing elevate or assist in the production?

If you didn't have this thing, is the production impacted negatively?

Imagine how your production would be in the end if you didn't have this thing.

You might discover you don't need it at all. Or you might discover you will! Either way, it's always important to ask some questions and think about it consciously before getting the thing just because you have the money. There's nothing creative about that.

DOCUMENTARIES

This is a genre that certainly requires planning, but one that has its own lifeforce. Sometimes it can take years to complete a documentary. Especially if you're following a living person or storyline like a trial or healing treatment.

I once directed a "year in the life" documentary about renowned belly dance and burlesque star Princess Farhana (aka Pleasant Gehman) and devoted an entire year to follow her around worldwide. We didn't film her every single day. It was more like a week here, a weekend there, a Belly Dance Cruise this month, followed by another event the next. On and on for months and months. Traveling around to where she performed and interviewing fellow artists and dancers in that field was exciting.

Though the same steps apply and the need to plan ahead vitally important, scheduling a documentary is very different than planning a narrative film.

SHORTS

Just because it takes less days to produce a short film, a web series, educational clip, corporate film, or a commercial, there is no less reason to also plan ahead and be vigilant about the organization for any kind of production. Regardless of size or length, the Master Plan is a one size fits all methodology.

WORKING WITHOUT A SCRIPT

One of the most rewarding and magical experiences I've ever had was directing EL GANZO starring Susan Traylor and Anslem Richardson in Los Cabos, Mexico.

The way in which we filmed it was a first for me. We had no real screenplay. There were some scenes sketched out, a very specific plotline to follow, but no real knowledge of how exactly it would all come together.

The decision to approach a film this way was inspired by my friend, the late great movie star Karen Black. For those of you who don't know Karen's work, I recommend you put this book down at once and watch DAY OF THE LOCUST, FIVE EASY PIECES,

NASHVILLE, FIRECRACKER, and THE GREAT GATSBY. Then resume reading.

Karen told me a secret before she died. She said, "If you want to know how it feels to really be alive, to really be present, you'll find that in the unknown. In not knowing. Because if you know about the road, you know that there's a curve coming up. You know there's a tree around the next corner, then a town after that. If you're going down a road you already know, you aren't really present."

Then her eyes lit up like a fire, "But, if you've never been down that road before, you don't know what's coming up. You don't know what's around the next turn. So, you have to be really present. Really focused. Because you don't know. And in that place of not knowing...it's the most magical place to be."

I decided to make EL GANZO in that mindset.

We filmed the movie in sequence. Most films are made totally out of order, but in this case, we planned ahead and made sure it was possible to organize the filming to be in sequence with the story.

Each morning we would meet in the lobby of our hotel to go over the game plan and what scenes we'd be doing that day. We didn't know where the scenes would take place or how the scenes would unfold. We only knew we needed to hit this list of targets for the day.

We went to a nearby village and filmed the first two scenes.

There were some cool shops around the plaza and we decided to take a little break. At some point that day we were to film a scene where Susan's character was to change clothes. We imagined finding a little stand selling textiles, or who knows. We would improvise, however it was to be, that this need to change costume made sense given our storyline and location.

When I walked into a shop to look for some trinkets, I noticed a small rack of clothing which had some shirts and dresses which looked exactly like Susan's costume we had in our gear. I asked the shopkeeper, Magdalena, if she would allow us to film a scene in her shop. She glowed with excitement and invited us in.

While we were filming that scene, I realized I couldn't take my eyes off Magdalena. Her energy was captivating, and her gaze stunned me. I couldn't help but get her in the film somehow. We asked her if she might also like to appear in the scene as the Shopkeeper. She didn't hesitate.

Because we had no script, we told her to just go with the flow and improvise. What came out of her mouth was poetry. It was as if it had been scripted. When we finished, we thanked her immensely. As the crew was packing up, I overheard her say, "That was so fun, it's been a long time since I was in front of a camera."

"Magdalena," we asked, "who are you?"

Turns out she was a famous News Anchor in Mexican television. No wonder she was so natural in front of the camera and spoke with such elegance and authority.

After that glorious moment, we cherished it and got back in the production van to drive to the next location. On the way we realized we were tired and hungry and needed to stop for food. The next thing we needed to do was film a car wreck. Or maybe we would come across a small child playing with toy cars, and we could ask the child to pretend there's a car accident with his toys. We didn't know what we would find, but we needed to have Susan's character see or hear "an incident" which would jog her memory of having been in a car accident. Yes, I know... We picked a storyline that wasn't the easiest thing to do under these circumstances.

Finally, we arrived at this little shack to have lunch. I stayed outside to have a cigarette before going in. The crew said, "There's no time to smoke, hurry up!" I ignored them and stayed put.

Seconds later, a metallic noise caught my attention and I turned my head to the left. A few yards right in front of me was a wrecked car with a smashed windshield. It was being strapped up to be pulled down the side of the hill—any moment! I shouted, "GET THE CAMERA! SUSAN! ANSLEM! HURRY!"

We got it.

We filmed the scene and it played as though we'd planned it all along.

That's how it was to film EL GANZO. That was an example of just one day. Each filming day was just as exciting and totally as magical as that day.

Now, let me say that we were impeccably organized. Making a feature film without a traditional screenplay could be a recipe for disaster. Everyone in EL GANZO is so incredibly talented that you'd never know it wasn't scripted. When creating the Master Plan for that shoot in particular, many careful observations had to be incorporated. Extra time was added so we could allow the secrets inside the unknown to come forth and find us.

STEVE BALDERSON

EPILOGUE

I sat down to interview Master Cinematographer Hanuman Brown-Eagle. This is what he had to say about the following topics.

Balderson: "How do you work creatively within restraints?"
Brown-Eagle: "First, I have to identify what is the one thing that is out of my control. For example, the sunlight is coming through the window and there's no practical way to cover the windows because they're so big. So now I know that I need to base all of my decisions off this one thing I can't control—the sun coming through the window. It might be that I could control the sun coming through the window. If I can, I do that. Then I say, now that I've controlled the sun coming through the window what is the one thing I can't control now? There might be a chandelier that has orange-colored lights, and I don't have access to change the lightbulbs, so I need to make all my decisions based on that one thing that's out of my control. Always start with the one thing that's out of your control and build from there."

"Do you remember when you first saw The Master Plan?"

"The most obvious difference between a master plan and a shot list or a call sheet is that it has the times listed in 15-minute increments. So, you can easily see what time of day something is happening as opposed to moving forward hoping to get it all done.

"What usually always happens is people end up spending the first two thirds of the day on one third of the shots. And only after that, people realize they don't have time to finish the rest of the day because you spent too much time on the first part. The Master Plan is an obvious way to predetermine how much time you're going to allocate for each scene that you have to get done that day. The first time we worked together, and I saw the Master Plan, I think what struck me immediately is that this is the solution to avoid all that. It sounds so obvious when I'm saying it out loud."

"Why do you think that nobody's done it before?"

"It doesn't make any sense. It doesn't make any logical sense to me because it should be an obvious connection. Time is the one thing that's always missing. We usually have a call sheet that lists what scenes we're going to film. But there's very little thought put into how long it will take to film them. It's kind of arbitrary. Because of that, we move at a certain pace for the first eight hours of the day and then we move twice as fast for the last four hours trying to catch up to all this stuff that we didn't plan accordingly for."

"Have you ever worked on anything that does incorporate time? Or take actual clock time into consideration?"

"No," he said, "I don't think so. No."

"What about the Master Plan is most beneficial to your particular job as a Cinematographer?"

"I appreciate there being actual expectations. Usually when working with the First AD, it's a fun game to play to try to stay ahead of the First AD and be ready before they are. That's a fun game to play but it's usually totally arbitrary. People generally take as long as they need and then we start working. Actually, having a clear expectation on paper of what time we're going to start shooting gives me the chance to help us stay on schedule and to know where we stand throughout the day.

"Honestly, it isn't about my having access to that information as much as it's about working for somebody who's given it that thought. I wouldn't necessarily even need to see the Master Plan, but if the person in charge doesn't make one then they probably don't know what the hell they're doing. The Master Plan is the chance for the person in charge to figure out how the day is going to go before it begins. If those in charge don't do that work, then I know it isn't going to be easy for me. I like to know what's coming up so that I can prepare for it. Some special needs for that particular scene or that particular day. Without the Master Plan, I might not know about that. Having a Master Plan informs me what is needed and when."

"Why is planning ahead important to you?"

"I think it makes it more fun. I think the more planning ahead that you do, the more fun you have when you're doing the work. Execution is more fun if there's not the burden of trying to figure out what it is that we need in order to execute. Otherwise, you're always trying to catch up as opposed to just being prepared. It's the difference between studying for a test and not studying for a test. When you study for a test, you've got all the answers and when you don't, you're sweating.

"In the first decade of my career in production, I obsessively planned and did lighting diagrams for everything ahead of time. I remember one of the things that I would do is go through the shot list and divide the amount of time that we had. So just for my own sake, I would say, 'Okay we have this much time to get this shot, and this much time to get that shot.' It was a similar idea to the Master Plan. I didn't want it to be my fault if the production fell behind. I was doing it for my own sense of wellbeing."

"How have productions worked for years without The Master Plan?"

"That's all a credit to the First AD. It's much more difficult, however, because it's all happening on set in real time, as opposed to being thought out in advance. The Master Plan allows a person to decide ahead of time, for example, what are the least important scenes so we might schedule those at the end of the day, in case we don't have time to film them. Whereas those kinds of compromises are usually made very rushed, in the moment, and not necessarily well thought out."

"Do you see any negativity to having a Master Plan?"

"Oh," Hanuman's face lit up. "I can play devil's advocate! The Master Plan might restrict creativity because it doesn't allow for the freedom to experiment and see what happens. It says you must be done with this scene in the next 30 minutes. That kind of structure doesn't allow time for Kubrick and The Cruises to find whatever they found after three days of hammering into the same scene over and over. Well, that's not the Master Plan that's creating the time limits, it's the budget that's creating the time limits. Okay, it isn't a good argument because you could have a Master Plan that simply says, 'Okay for the next three days we'll be shooting this one scene.' It's more of a function of the budget than it is a function of the Master Plan. I think the Master Plan is revolutionary, but it's also not complicated. It's kind of obvious and everyone should just do it."

STEVE BALDERSON

APPENDIX

BONUS: COMMUNICATION

Understanding the following information is useful when communicating with anybody, anywhere.

The DNA of communication is made up of words, the tonality used when expressing those words, and your physiology during the expression of those words. What's so mind-blowing is that only seven percent of communication is made up of words. Hitchcock always said that you should be able to watch the movie without the sound and still know what's going on. That's because 55% of communication is physiology alone. And then 38% is tonality.

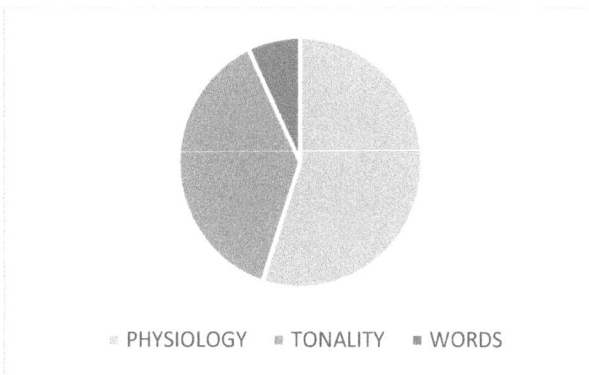

⬚ PHYSIOLOGY   ▪ TONALITY   ▪ WORDS

PHYSIOLOGY (55%) includes

Posture

Facial expression and blinking

Gesture

Breathing

TONALITY (38%) includes

Voice: Tone (pitch, high/low)

Tempo (speed, fast/slow)

Timbre (quality, crisp/raspy)

Volume (loudness)

WORDS (7%) include

Predicates

Content (Big picture/vague VS specific and detailed)

If everybody understood this it would revolutionize interpersonal communication with any relationship (family, spouse, friends, boss-employee, everybody). Almost everyone has received an email or text message without adequate or specific words, and sometimes the wrong words altogether. It's no wonder there are so many misunderstandings in communication when people miss out on the voice and body language. Text messages and emails are only operating at 7% effective communication levels.

Another thing to understand: the meaning of communication is not what you're saying. The meaning of communication is what the Other person hears. For instance, you might know exactly what you're thinking. You have an exact picture in your mind, you know exactly what you're talking about. When you pick words to describe that image, the other person is not privy to the image in your head. They only take in the words you use and notice your body language or tonality. They have no idea what's going on inside your mind.

A lot of people don't realize this because they think that the way they're seeing the world is obviously the way that everybody else is seeing it. At this point in the book, you know—no two people see the same thing the same way. Even so, many people cannot imagine that others understand things in a totally different way, with a completely different meaning. You can even see this in the words I have used in this paragraph. It is full of "visual" words. "Seeing the world" or "no two people see the same thing..." My father, who is auditory would have written "no two people hear things the same." Remember this when you are communicating.

We talked about this earlier a little bit, but I'll elaborate further. Take an event or situation that's happening nearby. This experience goes into us by way of the five senses. Visual, auditory, kinesthetic (feel), gustatory (taste) and olfactory (smell). And once this information is inside our minds we delete, distort and generalize it. These are our filters for the incoming information.

This is also made up of time and space. Where are we? What is the language? The words? Our culture? Our own memories of similar situations? Our own decisions made throughout our entire lives up until today. Our own values and beliefs. Our own attitude in general about whatever the experience is.

When you are having a conversation or experiencing an event, the words and experience itself passes through a filter. Every living person has their own unique filter. Even if someone else grew up in the very same house or neighborhood you did, their filter is a different make and model than yours. No two people have the same filter.

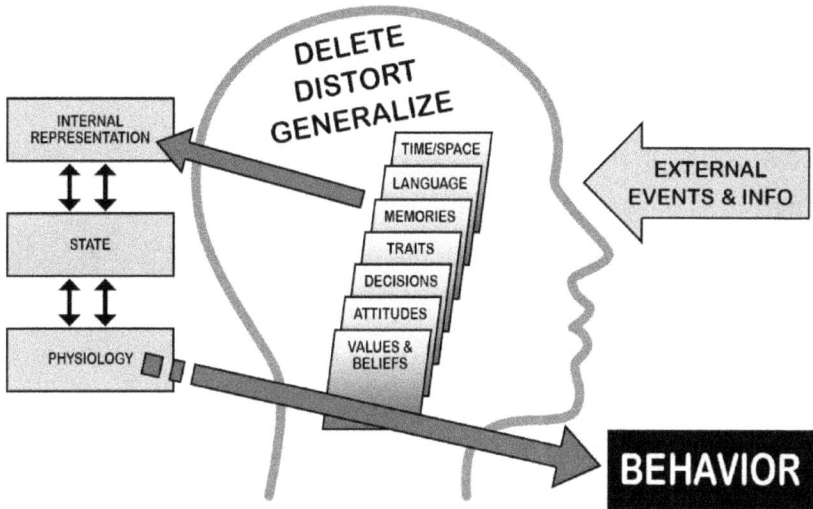

Your own values, beliefs, attitudes, decisions and memories are then turned into your internal representations of the external event or situation. All humans go through this process whether you know about it, understand it, choose to disregard it, or not.

After we've made an internal representation of what's going on, then that internal representation is going to put us into an emotional state. The way we process this information will inform and effect our psychology, physiology and our state of being based on what the filter has made into the internal representation, which will be different in every person.

Another thing: this process happens in a fraction of a millisecond. The results come out in our behavior whether they are action or verbal.

Effective communication is a lot more complicated than simply deciding what to say to someone. Every single person's externalized and internalized experience is different. If I speak English, and you don't, no matter how loud I say it, you won't understand what I'm saying. You might understand that my tone is angry or in need of help, and my face might look frightened, but you likely won't understand my words because I'm not speaking your language. Even if you do, in fact, speak the same language, communication between two people is frequently ineffective.

I know film directors who turn to the set dresser and say, "That looks ugly. I said to make it beautiful."

Those words are very general. There's nothing specific about the word beautiful. One person's idea of beautiful is another person's idea of ugly, and there are a million ways to communicate in between the two. If the director is mentally picturing a green vase and has associated the word beautiful with the color green, the director should specify and communicate this. No one else knows what he's thinking. Many people are certain and clear about whatever they are imagining in their minds. Sometimes these images are so clear and obvious to the thinker it is as if everyone else can see the image too.

The DNA of communication is made up of seven percent words, 38% tonality and 55% physiology. Once you know this and understand it, only then do you realize that 93% of meaningful communication is unconscious. It doesn't matter if you say, "I'm fine, thank you," while you're sitting in a corner with a scowl on your face. The other person will know that you are definitely not "fine."

Now that you know this, you will see it everywhere you look. You can use this knowledge to benefit your relationships, working environments and experiences every day.

ABOUT THE AUTHOR

Preeminent film critic Roger Ebert gave Steve's film *Firecracker*, starring Karen Black and Mike Patton, a Special Jury Award on his annual Best Films of the Year list. His first film *Pep Squad* premiered at the Cannes Film Festival and became a 90s cult classic. The U.S. Library of Congress selected his film *The Casserole Club*, starring Kevin Richardson of the Backstreet Boys, for its permanent collection. Steve ranks #47 on the IMDb's Top 100 Gay and Lesbian Directors working today. His first book, "Filmmaking Confidential," debuted as an Amazon and Audible best-seller. He is a contributor to The Advocate and MovieMaker magazines and has been a guest lecturer at the University of California Los Angeles (UCLA).

BOOKS BY THE AUTHOR

"Filmmaking Confidential"
(2020, Dikenga Books)

"How to Find Investors"
(2021, Dikenga Books)

"PHONE SEX"
(2021, Dikenga Books)

www.SteveBalderson.com
www.FilmmakingConfidential.com
www.DIKENGA.com